Dear Chiefs, We need to talk:

A No BS Guide For Fire Families

How to navigate, support and love a first responder and not lose yourself in the process.

By Audra Carrion + Chelsi McFadden

This book is dedicated to all the signifigant others and spouses who came before us and were left in the wild without a guide on how to navigate this first responder family life . Special thanks to our firefighter husbands Damien and Cameron who support us, and let us speak our truth every day with unwavering support.

Welcome to a simplified guide to being a fire family.

This no BS guide will provide you with the tools you need to succeed in your relationship, how to support your partner without losing yourself in the process.

Loving a firefighter is not always easy. It's messy and complicated some days. There will be times when your partner is called away on duty, leaving you to fend for yourself. There will be times when they are exposed to danger and trauma. And there will be times when they are simply exhausted from their work.

We are so excited to walk you through our tried and true techniques to supporting our firefighters AND our relationships. We want you to read this guide with an open mind and we encourage you to tweak these ideas to fit your own relationship.

XO

Audra + Chelsi

So you want to be a firefighter…

Let’s start with the basics for the firefighter. How to prioritize family life when you are first starting your career. In the next few pages we’re speaking specifically to the firefighter.

Understand your signifigant other

You can only grow your relationship if you are attentive to the needs of your family at home. One way to understand exactly what your family needs is to ASK. Ask your spouse how you can help when you're home. Take initiative on basic tasks. Offer to do groceries, drive kids to sports, walk the dogs, etc. Find out what your spouse needs and check in often on what else you can do to participate.

Prioritize your time at home

Make a conscious effort to prioritize your time at home. When you're off duty, dedicate quality time to your spouse and children. Put away distractions and be fully present. Plan activities, outings, and family meals to strengthen your bond and create lasting memories. Set aside regular blocks of uninterrupted time for family interactions.

Share the mental load

Being married to a firefighter often places a significant mental load on the spouse. You can alleviate the mental load by openly communicating, sharing their experiences, and seeking support together. By empathizing and actively participating in discussions, you create a supportive environment, strengthening the relationship while navigating challenges.

Connect often

Find a way to connect with each other that works for you. Plan a date. Even in your backyard. Send a quick text on duty. Share a funny meme, send a joke or just tell them you love them. Let them know you're thinking of them often.

Include your spouse

Involve your spouse in your firefighting career as much as possible Share stories about your experiences, involve them in department events or gatherings, and give them opportunities to learn about your work. By including your partner, you create a sense of shared purpose and encourage their active participation, leading to a stronger bond between you and a deeper understanding of your profession.

Schedule your study time

Firefighting academies or promotional exams often require extensive studying. To prevent it from encroaching on your family time, sit down with your spouse and schedule dedicated study time that works for the family. By establishing a routine and allowing your partner to support you during these times, you can strike a balance between your career development and family responsibilities.

REST!

Resting. Is. Important!
Rest allows your mind and body to rest. Talk to your spouse about how you slept on shift and communicate your need for a nap. Go to bed early.

Show appreciation and Validate Your Spouse

It doesn't have to be extravagant. Show gratitude, participate in shared responsibilities, and prioritize their personal well-being, nurturing a strong and supportive relationship amidst the demands of your career.

Help your spouse find support

Invite other firefighter families over. Ask a family member to take the kids one day. By building a support network, you can help your spouse feel less isolated, provide them with a sense of community, and offer mutual support as you navigate the demands of your firefighting career together.

Set yourself and your family up for success

- Find your EAP or mental health information and write it down for your family.
- Understand your retirement, your health benefits, your salary schedule. Add your spouse, your children, and beneficiaries.
- Get life insurance.
- Sit down with a financial planner.
- FInd a buddy at work to be your spouse's liason should something happen to you on duty.

Keep notes of your benefits, important information, and your EAP here:

For spouses and partners of firefighters and first responders

Being the spouse or partner of a firefighter or first responder is an extraordinary role filled with unique challenges and rewards. This section explores the dynamics, offers guidance on communication and emotional well-being, and provides insights into the complexities of being a first responder partner.

What to expect when your partner gets hired with a fire department

Academy

Keep in mind that each department is different. Not all departments have an academy. Some who get hired have already done a fire academy through a community college or private entity. Some are put through a "mini" academy. If your partner does go through a full academy, expect 16-20 weeks of grueling work, exhaustive studying, and being generally tapped out of everything else except for the academy.

Moreover, the scheduling dynamics during this time differ from what you may be accustomed to. Long days for your partner become the norm, sometimes extending into nights. This can mean prolonged periods where you'll be without their physical presence, and you'll need to adapt to being alone more and sleeping alone. Mentally preparing for these changes is essential to maintaining a solid and supportive relationship during this challenging period.

Probation

Congratulations, your firefighter made it through the academy! Now get ready for probation!!
Probation is typically 12-18 months but can vary with departments. Every new hire is conditional until they pass probation. Probationary firefighters must prove to the department that they are fit for duty and can do the job they were hired for. This can be a very stressful time for your firefighter as the probationary period is a critical phase in their career.

A few things to note for your firefighter:
Probies typically don't get to sit down for the first year or more.
Probies have to do a lot of cleaning and extra house duties in most departments.

The seasoned fire personnel love to mess with a proby, so get ready for some light-hearted fun and pranks.
**Note: hazing of any kind is unacceptable during probation or at any time. No firefighter should be made to feel unsafe at work.

Shift schedule and vacations

Firefighters often go through a shift bidding process where they rank their preferences for shifts based on their seniority. The more senior firefighters have priority in choosing their preferred shifts. This system recognizes their years of service and experience within the department. However, it's important to note that not all departments allow complete freedom in shift selection, and a lottery or rotation system may be in place to maintain balance.

Similar to shift bidding, the allocation of vacation time is often done based on seniority. The vacation bidding process may involve selecting specific dates or time blocks. In some departments, this is done a year in advance.

Understanding the department's policies and working together to align personal schedules can help mitigate potential conflicts and ensure a better work-life balance.

Promotion

Promotions within a fire department are typically based on varying factors, including years of service, performance evaluations, specialized training, educational qualifications, leadership abilities, and successful completion of promotional exams. The specific promotion criteria and procedures may vary from one fire department to another. Any time your firefighter moves rank, they're back on probation.

During this probationary period, your firefighters will be closely observed and assessed by their superiors and peers. The duration of the probationary period may vary depending on the specific fire department and the rank being attained. It's usually anywhere from 6 months to a year. This can be a very stressful time for them as the probationary period is a critical phase in their career, and success during this time sets the tone for their future within the department.

As a partner, you can help by learning about the specific expectations, responsibilities, and stresses your spouse may be facing during this time. Sometimes just having someone to talk to can be a great relief. Be patient and understanding if they are fatigued, irritable, or preoccupied with work-related matters. Let them know you are there for them. Most importantly, ask them what they need from you to feel supported and discuss how you can be there for each other during this crucial time.

Basic things you need to know about the work of a firefighter

Budget for station meals!

Firefighters are gone for days on end and don't always bring food from home. They usually eat on their own for breakfast and lunch. They take turns making meals for dinner and they LOVE to show off. Meals and snacks add up quick so find a budget that works for both you and your firefighter. The average week for firefighter food is about $60.

Be prepared for plans to change.

Overtime and mandos are inevitable. You will rarely get advanced notice. Be ready to attend the holiday party by yourself. Be prepared to cancel last minute or to do things solo. Try not to take it out on your firefighter - it's just part of the job.

Your family and friends won't always get it.

It's a "if you know, you know" situation. People outside of the firefighting community might not fully grasp the demands and challenges of the job.

Fire Season is a Myth

Modern firefighting is a year-round profession, and most departments handle all types of emergencies. With climate change and the urbanization of timberlands, the idea of a distinct fire season is outdated. The demands of the job are ongoing throughout the year.

The job will affect family dynamics.

The job is bound to affect family dynamics in some way. Whether it's the long hours, unpredictable schedules, massive overtime, or your firefighter's absence, these factors will impact your family. You may find yourself handling more of the day-to-day responsibilities and constantly adjusting to a new normal. This can sometimes lead to stress, especially when communication breaks down or important moments are missed. Remember, while the job is demanding, open communication and mutual understanding will help keep your family strong.

It takes a village

It takes a village to raise a first responder family. It's okay to ask for help and to recognize that your village might look different from the typical family's. Our support systems often include our trusty robot vacuums, paper plates for quick meals, the Uber delivery driver, and friendly neighbors who lend a hand when needed.

Nurturing Your Relationship as a First Responder Partner

Prioritize Quality Time

It's easy to get caught up in the demands of first responder life, but carving out quality time for your relationship is crucial. Whether it's a weekly date night or a cozy evening in, make intentional efforts to reconnect and nurture your love.

Practice Active Listening

Effective communication is the backbone of a thriving relationship. Learn the art of active listening—giving your partner your undivided attention, empathizing, and validating their experiences. By truly hearing each other, you can strengthen your emotional connection.

Foster Emotional Resilience

Being a first responder partner requires emotional resilience. Find healthy coping mechanisms to navigate the stress and uncertainty that can accompany the role. Engage in activities that promote emotional well-being, such as journaling, practicing mindfulness, or seeking professional support when needed. Taking care of your emotional health will strengthen your ability to support your first responder and maintain a thriving relationship.

Cultivate Self-Care Rituals

As a partner, it's essential to prioritize self-care. Develop personal rituals that replenish your energy and promote well-being. Whether it's indulging in a hobby, practicing mindfulness, or exercising, taking care of yourself will enable you to be there for your first responder with renewed strength.

Celebrate Milestones, Big and Small

Amidst the challenges, don't forget to celebrate the victories—both big and small! From successfully handling a difficult call to simply making it through a hectic week, acknowledge and appreciate the resilience and dedication of your first responder. Every milestone reached is a testament to your unwavering support.

Foster Open Communication

Create a safe space for open and honest conversations. Encourage your first responder to share their experiences, emotions, and concerns. Show empathy and understanding while also expressing your own needs and feelings. By fostering open communication, you can strengthen your emotional connection and build trust.

Practice Gratitude

In the midst of the chaos, practicing gratitude can bring immense joy and appreciation to your relationship. Express your gratitude for your first responder's service and commitment. Small gestures, heartfelt notes, and words of appreciation go a long way in nurturing your bond.

Never Forget Your Why

In moments of difficulty, always remember your why—the love, respect, and admiration that brought you together in the first place. Remind yourself of the incredible difference your first responder makes in the lives of others. Together, you are a team, and your unwavering support can conquer any obstacle.

Hard Truths Every First Responder Spouse or Significant Other Needs to Hear

Resilience is learned.

Being in a relationship with a first responder is not easy. There will be days that you just want to throw in the towel. But, it is at these moments that you will discover your inner strength. Resilience is not something you're born with, but it's a skill that you can learn and develop as you go through life. It's all about being able to bounce back from tough situations and using them as opportunities to learn and grow.

You often will be alone, but you don't have to be lonely

There are plenty of ways to enjoy your own company and find joy and satisfaction in solitude. You can indulge in your hobbies, explore new interests, try out new recipes, read a good book, practice meditation or yoga, or simply spend time in nature. You can also connect with people online or over the phone, reach out to friends or family, or volunteer for a cause that you feel passionate about. Remember, being alone doesn't have to be a negative experience—it can be an opportunity for growth, introspection, and self-discovery.

Uncertainty becomes a constant companion

Being in a relationship with a first responder means embracing a lifestyle that is often marked by unpredictability. From sudden schedule changes to unexpected emergencies, uncertainty becomes a regular part of your life. This constant state of flux can be challenging to navigate, but it also teaches you the importance of adaptability and resilience. Embracing the uncertainty together can strengthen your bond and help you face the future with courage and resilience.

You will face difficulties that other couples never experience

From changing work schedules to potential danger, there are unique difficulties that come with being a first responder spouse. You need to be prepared for the unexpected and see the world from a different perspective.

You have to be strong and self-reliant

As a first responder spouse, you have to be able to take care of yourself. You need to have the courage to stand up for yourself when your partner is away and to deal with any challenges that come your way.

You will always worry

There will be moments in your relationship with a first responder when your heart may feel heavy with worry. As much as their job may fill you with pride, it can also bring about moments of concern. Remember, it's okay to feel a mix of emotions, and by acknowledging and accepting them, you can navigate through them with understanding and support.

You may feel like you come second to their job

Being a first responder spouse means sometimes feeling like you come second to the job. But remember, it doesn't mean you're any less valued or loved. It's a result of the unique demands and responsibilities.

Your feelings matter

Never forget that your feelings matter and that being in a relationship with a first responder can often be rewarding, but it comes with its own unique set of challenges. That's why the spouse or partner of a first responder needs to understand the hard truths of the job. It's only by having a realistic understanding of the situation that a relationship can be healthy and thrive amid these demands.

How To Help Your First Responder With The "Tricky Transition" From Work To Home

Check in on the way home

Send a quick text, or give them a call and let them know your plan for the day and ask what they need from you.

Rest or walk

Did they have a restless shift? Let them rest. Are they feeling ok? Take a 20-minute walk to re set and decompress.

Allow them some time to adjust

Don't expect them to come home and just GO. They need a moment to adjust their mind and body to their surroundings at home.

Work together

Communication and working together will smooth the transition. Try not to dump and run. Don't expect them to handle everything the moment they get home.

Reconnect

Try to reconnect with your partner as soon as possible. Hold their hand over a cup of coffee, give a 1 minute hug. Touch is an easy way to reconnect and ground both people.

Timing and mood

RIght after a shift is not the time to be making big decisions. Choose a time when you are both relaxed and available to discuss.

Make a plan

Try to agree on a routine that will help them transition home more smoothly. Keep in mind the routine may need to be adjusted based on their shift.

Make a list

Keep a list of things you want to tell your first responder about. Jot down key dates, or information you need to share. Things that happened while they were away. Put it in your notes app or keep a running journal you can keep notes in for them.

When all else fails, sleep on it.

If it's not important, let them sleep on it. Nap, or their first night home. Give yourselves time to get back in your groove before you share your thoughts.

What to do when your firefighter is on an out-of-county incident

how to handle those long days without your fire fighter

Take a break from social media

Seeing everyone else's "perfect" lives can add stress. Disconnect when you need to focus on creating a routine that works for you.

Skip the scanner chatter or news updates

It's tempting to stay tuned in, but constant updates can add worry. Trust your partner to reach out when they can; give yourself permission to step back.

Prioritize fun, not perfection

Let go of 'perfect' routines. Choose fun when you can—game nights, messy art, or simple meals. These moments can help lighten the mood and lift everyone's spirits.

Invest in your mental wellness

It's okay to feel lonely, resentful, or burnt out—name those feelings when they come up. Then, try to reframe them: connect with someone, find purpose in your support, or acknowledge that these feelings are a natural part of your experience.

For the default parents: lean on simplifying

Being the primary parent means finding ways to simplify—easy dinners, relaxed routines, and letting some things slide are all okay! Give yourself grace where possible.

Set Boundaries Where You Can

Not every chore or commitment needs to be handled right now. Set limits on what you take on and let go of the small stuff to keep your balance.

Remember, your village is whatever you make it

Support can come from anywhere—a quick call to a friend, neighbors who lend a hand, the Uber driver delivering dinner, or even the robo vac doing the heavy lifting on the floors. Embrace whatever lightens the load!

What to do after a critical incident

HOW TO SUPPORT EACH OTHER AS YOU HEAL

Do they want to talk?

Ask your first responder if they want to talk about the incident. If they say no, don't force it. Let them know you are there for them if/when they are ready.

Reestablish routines

There is solace in the mundane rhythm of your everyday life. Get back on track with work, school and playdate schedules. You can start by writing down what your routine was before. If going into it again all at once seems like a lot then try implementing a part of your routine day by day.

Give yourself permission to heal

Even if people around you are still recovering, it's okay if you are ready to move on. It is okay for you to rebuild and get back to normal. If you find that it is too much ask for help. Your department more than likely has resources available to you and if not, there are organizations out there ready to help. If that seems extreme, send us a dm, we'd be happy to talk with you!

Don't be helpless

You may feel helpless, but you are not. Sometimes the way to get happy is to make someone else smile. You can challenge that helpless feeling and kick it straight to the curb. You can volunteer to help at a local food bank or shelter.

If volunteering isn't your thing, there is always the power of kindness. Small gestures of kindness like smiling at a stranger, holding a door open for someone and even offering to help your elderly neighbor get her groceries inside are all ways to make you feel helpful.

Seek help if you need it

It may be time to seek professional help if you or your First Responder experience any of the following:

1. You still aren't feeling better after 6 weeks.
2. You have trouble functioning at home or work
3. You can't sleep or are being woken by nightmares.
4. You are having suicidal thoughts
5. You are avoiding more and more things relating to the incident.

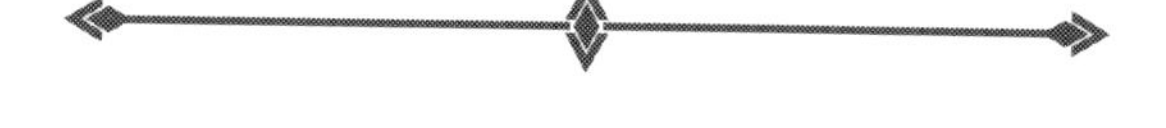

Prioritizing self-care for default parents in first responder families

Treat self-care like any other appointment by scheduling it into your calendar. Have a weekly or monthly check-in with yourself to evaluate what you need.
Fill it with things that bring you comfort or joy, such as favorite books, candles, or skincare products. Keep a smaller version handy for moments of stress.
Take short breaks throughout the day for deep breathing, stretching, or a quick walk. even praying or meditating throughout the day can be a huge help!

Identify tasks that can be delegated to others, whether it's with family members or through hiring help. Don't hesitate to reach out to friends or family for support.
Hint: Sometimes the uber eats delivery guy is the mvp of team first responder family!

Set clear boundaries around work, family time, and personal time to prevent burnout.
Communicate these boundaries to your partner and family members.

Be Kind to yourself. Recognize that it's okay to need and take time for yourself. Self-compassion can help reduce feelings of guilt.
Replace negative thoughts with affirmations and self-kindness.
Make time for hobbies and activities that bring you joy, whether they're long-time favorites or new interests. Engaging in creative outlets like writing, crafting, or exploring new passions can be both therapeutic and fulfilling.

Join support groups or communities for first responder spouses to share experiences and get advice, and stay connected with friends and family for extra emotional support and socialization.

Consider seeing a therapist or counselor to work through stress or emotional challenges.
Life coaching can aslo help you set and achieve personal goals.

What to do after a critical incident

Helping eachother through a line of duty death

Be patient and understanding

Understand that grief is complex. Be patient with their emotions and provide them with space to express themselves. They may experience a range of emotions. Offer understanding and reassurance, even when they are struggling.

Remember and celebrate

Share memories and stories about the fallen comrade. Honor their legacy together and keep their spirit alive.

Offer practical support

Help with everyday tasks, like cooking meals or running errands, to ease their burden during this difficult time.

Limit exposure to news and media coverage

Excessive news consumption can bombard you with distressing images, stories, and speculations, intensifying feelings of grief and anxiety. Give yourself space to process emotions without additional triggers.

Process your emotions

Remember, you are also grieving. It's essential to prioritize self-care and nurture your own well-being.

Stay Connected

Maintain regular communication and check-ins. Let them know that you are there for them, no matter what.

For more information on how to navigate being in a relationship with a first responder tune into our podcast on any streaming app. Stay in touch by joining our social media pages and our website dearchiefs.com where you can join our mailing list and read more about our lives as first responder spouses.

Stay tuned for more stories coming soon.

Suicide Prevention Resources

If you need help, information or anything regarding mental health,please use any of the information below:

Text 988

Call 1-800-273-TALK(8255)

Text BRAVE to 741 741 for a trained crisis counselor

Go to the nearest emergency room.

Ask someone for help

Made in the USA
Las Vegas, NV
08 December 2024

13635159R00017